AS CLOSE AS I CAN

AS CLOSE AS I CAN

Poems by

Toni Stern

CircleStar
SANTA BARBARA

Copyright © 2017 by Toni Stern
All Rights Reserved

Published in the United Sates
by Circle Star Press,
Santa Barbara, California

Library of Congress Cataloging-in-Publication Data

Stern, Toni
As Close as I Can.
Poems
1. Title
ISBN 978-0-692-93994-9

Printed in the United States of America
10 9 8 7 6 5 4 3 2 1

Cover design by John Balkwill and Trish Reynales
Cover photo of Toni Stern by Cheryl Finnegan
Book Design by Lumino Press

To the Reader

It isn't ever delicate to live.
—Kay Ryan, "Spiderweb"

CONTENTS

I

Hwy 154—Between Two Fires   17
Childhood's Promise   18
I Don't   19
Pine Sol™   20
Vera's Not a Mirror She's a Window   21
She   22
Familiars   23
Two to Tangle   24
Turning the Tables   25
Sometimes   26
Thinking of You   27
Yes, Petunia   28
Everything is Singing   29
Ablutions   30
Young Guns   31
Self-Portraits   32
John and Joe   33
Everywhere at Once   34
Ruth   35

II

Like That 39

To a Rose 40

Progenation 41

The Trip 42

Having It All 43

IEDs 44

Untitled 46

Anhedonia 47

The Unhurried Dead 48

Give Us This Day 49

Proof of Life 50

Financial Security 51

Backbone 52

The Trouble With War 53

Where Would We Be Without You 54

To a Chicken 55

Chosen* 56

Coyote Blues 57

State of Emergency 58

The Paved Road 59

III

As Close as I Can 63

Reality Check 64

Mixed Messages 65

Aviso 66

Dream Job 67

Four A.M. 68

Weight 69

Away From Here 70

I Know I Know 71

Unreliable Witness 72

Pyrolysis 73

The Surrealist Poet 74

Thing 75

Numero Uno 76

Caprice 77

Fancy Free 78

Year's End 79

Ever Onward 80

I

Hwy 154—Between Two Fires

I can't adjudge which conceit
I subscribe to:
A man alone is in bad company, or,
Hell is other people.

Love! There's never enough.

The fountain burbles,
the clothes dryer thrums,
the brown towhee tweets
her widowed lament.

Each spring, our neighbors,
a pair of red-tails,
endure a traumatic nesting,
as the great horned owl
monitoring their downy chicks
bides his time.

In October, when the cows and calves
are separated, their lowing
unhinges the quiet.

My brown towhee is driving to town.
"Be safe," I tell him,
then add, "I mean it, be safe."

Childhood's Promise

Our goddaughter's here.
We bought her the two Barbies she'd been eyeing
as playmates for the one she already has.
When she asked which doll I liked best,
I was outmaneuvered.

I never liked dolls, save for an unclad
rubber baby I carted around
during my *Paper Moon* days.
I still have the photo I took of her,
posed on a meager patch of motel grass.

Off the road and enrolled in school,
I peopled my bed with stuffed animals—
In the morning they were always on the floor.

I loved my mother,
feared my brother,
grieved for my absent father.

I had a handwashing obsession
that lasted a day—
I did what all children do:

I endured.

I Don't

Stay in bed all morning
Lug iron
Believe in a higher authority
Despise the homeless
Speak in tongues
Photograph well
Paint barns for money
Cut flowers
Kill spiders
Spare earwigs
Collect snow globes
Sleep on my back,
Or water ski.

Pine Sol™

My exasperated husband
told me my negativity was tedious—
I suspected as much.

At least the floors are clean.

Vera's Not a Mirror She's a Window

Out early, now that summer's wilt is upon us,
we're headed for the park.

These days our favorite prey,
Vera's and mine,
is a young mother, toddler in tow,
happy to relieve the routine of parenting,
while her child and my pup
cautiously flirt with one another.

In the afternoon, lying on my desk,
sleepy-eyed Vera regards me with satisfaction.

She hears the truck before I do;
married life attends.
It's Passover and I've made potato pancakes.

She

tears into her chew toy
as if out for blood:
Vera, the mosquito in the room,
and me—

all out for blood.

Familiars

Sometimes I feign full-scale disinterest
in my husband, because he's wounded me
in some small way.
What spectacular foolishness—
punishing myself like that.

Two to Tangle

I love you unequivocally,
just not all the time.

Turning the Tables

I need to go out, but the wind,
blowing hard from the west, cows me.
There's so much to do.

I can do anything, I tell myself,
and for a heartbeat believe it.

When the sun sets and the wind dies down,
I'll go into the almost dark—
rake up the afternoon chaos,
water the tapped-out plants.

Tomorrow, in morning's hush,
I'll wake to a well-tended garden—
unconcerned with OCD,
revived in fact by the side of me,

that can't abide a mess.

Sometimes

the right word
is enough to staunch the bleeding.
Sometimes the right word,
at the right moment,
is enough.

THINKING OF YOU

Everything's different
now that you're gone,
yet nothing has changed.

Yes, Petunia

"Yes, my Petunia?"
he sometimes says,
when he's pleased with me
and I've called to him
from the next room—
the house humming with
goodwill.

So I ask for ____, and then
four more,
then more and more I'm
jonesing for. I wear him out
with (more) demands,
he (truly) tosses up
his hands,
pulls away—and
well he can!

Sorry, sorry, my sweet
man,
I'll change my ways,
I know I can!

*Don't tell my fans what an ass I
am,*

a recidivist, self-indulgent
ham.

Everything is Singing

Aloe vera blossoming
  crimson in the heat,
in a corner of a garden
  no one visits.

Ablutions

Skin as thin as puzzlement
adorn these thorny shins;
I see where this is going,
but I still don't quite believe it.

Young Guns

I said to Jack, "If *you*, meaning me,
champion *them*, meaning children,
forswearing all else,
they become fearless and foolhardy,
and could profit from a little
chastening."

"It's not that complicated," he said.
"They are here to mow you down,
and you my dear are here
to disappear."

Self-Portraits

depend upon the light,
and what you're looking for.
I used to look for flaws,
I don't do that anymore.

JOHN AND JOE

I had two invisible friends:
John and Joe.
Although they were identical,
I never considered them twins.
We were a triumvirate.

After school, we'd roughhouse
in front of the living-room TV,
my knees reddened from rolling around
on the coarse wool carpet.

One day, inexplicably, we stopped getting along,
and the last time I saw those two buzz-cut
little blond boys, we clobbered each other.
It was then that I met my two new friends—
Secretiveness and *Estrangement*.

What shall I say?
I love life,
even as it tears me to shreds.

Everywhere at Once

I don't know what luck is exactly,
but I know you need it, and
if, during the vertigo of youth,
I gained an edge,
it had little to do with ambition.

My mother treated me with diffidence
rather than affection and, in
our quiet household, I was left mostly alone.
When I was finally allowed a dog,
I felt whole.

From an early age, I liked boys
and could easily keep up with them.
Once, two young teens took my rough language
as an invitation to molest me—
When I told my father, I begged him,
"Don't tell mama!" I was convinced
she couldn't bear it.

I ask myself,
why these memories *now*?
I don't know—
as long as I'm still breathing,
so do they.

Ruth

I think I punched the little pigtailed girl
when she refused to be my best friend.
"I can't," she said, "I'm best friends with Esther."

According to Hasidic tradition,
remorse is a serious sin—
second only to sadness.

Maybe I just wanted to.

II

Like That

It's afternoon already,
and I just remembered to breathe—
Which is not to say
I'm not having any fun.

Some days I'm a wrathful Isaac Parker,
the hanging judge of Fort Smith, Arkansas;
others, well-tempered.

Will I have the courage after tea and ices, not
to force the situation to its crisis?

Inspired by injury,
I've been considering the body—
creating lists, like a bird-watcher:
scapula, traps, hip flexors, glutes, hamstrings, lats—
imagining a future perfect,
I *will have* healed.

"Never better," my father would say whenever
asked, generating a round of familial eye-rolling.
I think they wanted more from him—

He remained, though, until the end,
cheerfully disinterested in us.

To a Rose

I learned about the
crucifying climate of
Canadian convent life
in bits and pieces:
The cloistered nuns, the frigid attic,
and my four-year-old mother,
bearing her chronic cough,
warehoused by fickle, moneyed parents.

Coltish at times when she drank,
she was more often a reliquary of sadness.
Once (I was around ten),
I marveled as she danced on top of the piano
in an L.A. bar.
Unconcerned with my father and brother's
censorious looks,
she glowed—

is glowing still,
in *my* sadness.

Cheers, Mama.
"Here's to those who wish us well, and all the rest
can go to hell!"

PROGENATION

One sperm,
One egg—
Bob's your uncle.

The Trip

In the nineteen-sixties, I drove
to Sequoia National Park
with an attorney, I later learned was married—
a lying attorney, but that's another story.
We each took a tab of LSD
and, before it kicked in, smoked a joint.

At one point, he asked, "What if this is a movie?"
I thought, if you can't tell me who
the director is—I mean, *the* director—
I'm not interested.
First Cause or nothing!

There was a wonderful strangeness
to it all. Sex was out of the question,
though we did give it a try.

Everything was teeming.
The intervals between the trees as corporeal
as the giants themselves—
yet there was nothing to hold on to.

When ego abdicates its throne
it's easy to get lost: lost in the forest,
lost in the trees—

Thank god my mother made me
take a sweater.

Having It All

Her father teases, "Sharper than a serpent's tooth
is an ungrateful child." Her mother
never says this, though has reason to.
Her father is unquestionably her and her brother's
father, yet her brother names both his children
after her mother's lover.
Her mother's lover provides for the family in
various ways.

One night, her mother's lover castigates her
for her unwillingness to toil for him,
as her mother has. She never says
another civil word to her mother's lover.

After years away, her father returns and
her mother takes him in. When her mother dies,
her mother's lover evicts her father from the
apartment.

A widower at seventy-nine, he moves in
with her brother's ex-wife. She buys him a little
white dog, and he dies in his sleep twelve years later.

IEDs

Darling,
It's been a tough year;
turbulent and stubbornly sad.

Decades ago,
a man I was in thrall to had a wife.
Just before she took the Nembutal
(he later confided), he'd been savaging her
about her past.

Instead of dialing nine-one-one
when she lost consciousness,
he summoned his Beverly Hills celebrity doctor,
and in the time it took to cover their asses,
she died.

Bewitched as I was,
I rushed to his side.
The real, the unreal, he entreated.
The real, the real, the real.
I was twenty-two.

Darling,
This year at times seemed untenable.
I know you agree.

Now that we're friends again,
it's as if we've been acquitted
of a crime—

some random act of carelessness
we can't recall,

or ever
really
safeguard
against.

Untitled

She was quite the chatterbox
   before the violence—
Now, she rarely volunteers.

Besides, her sunniness,
   before the violence,
disgusted something in her.

That, she doesn't miss.

You can see the effort not to judge
leveling her eyes.

No lonelier than before—

probably still in shock.

Anhedonia

You've chosen the woman
with the beautiful name,
but she not you,
and all life's pleasures
are emptied of meaning.

When you tire of her treachery,
call me; we'll have a good laugh.

Who could have predicted
we never grow up.

The Unhurried Dead

I did everything right—
ate right, got plenty of sleep,
quit smoking years ago.

The others regard me impassively, but
I know what they're thinking:
*Bet she thought she was really something
when she was alive.
Now, she's one of us—*

Give Us This Day

I'm fine with being fearful
in those last few dying moments,
but *I'd* have drawn the line
at daily dread.

Proof of Life

The old woman, smelling of misfortune
regarded me,
"May I ask you a question?"
"Of course," I said.
"Do you believe in miracles?"
"No," I said.
Her eyes widened.
"Not even a maybe?"
"No," I said, "not even a maybe."

I thought: The affection I withhold from others,
I also deny myself.

The pharmacist waited for her to refocus,
and when she had, they sorted through the refills,
she couldn't afford them all, setting aside the ones she'd
"live without."

I thought: In order to believe in the miraculous, I'd
have to believe in its opposite, the unmiraculous.

I don't have the imagination for that.

Financial Security

A tough nut to swallow, but
Ya gotta eat.
Of course, if
You're truly hungry,
They close the pie shop,
Flip the sign:
CLOSED
Money is a cursed affair
When you need it,
An advantage if you don't.
It exploits weakness
And fortifies strength.
Who do you have to kill
To get some?
They say it can't buy love—
They're wrong of course.
It's yours for the price of a song.

BACKBONE

When the newswoman asked
the swamped-out Floridian
what he was going to do
now that he'd lost his house,
he grinned, "I got guns, food, and water."

The Trouble With War

He said, "I don't approve of women in combat."
She countered, "I don't approve of men in combat."
Sound the retreat!

Where Would We Be Without You

Sometimes humor is the only lifeline—
that's how grim it is sometimes.

Nothing like a soupçon of hellfire,
to inspire a psychic three-sixty.

To a Chicken

Thank you for the eggs,
And the mayonnaise;
Thank you for the thighs tonight,
I savored every oily bite.
Thank you for the giblets,
The sandwiches and soup;
Thanks for your docility
Inside the chicken coop.

Have you reckoned with the sound
Of footfalls on the frozen ground?

What white apron, streaked with red,
Inculcates your tiny head?
Thank you for the pâté—

Disgusting creatures, aren't we.

CHOSEN*

Loose cat on major league baseball field, plunges into the bleachers, careening through hundreds, no *thousands* of legs. Leaps into the arms of a fan, who holds him close, massaging his neck. An usher arrives to eject the cat. The cat gives the usher the stink eye, and the fan bids the man go away.

*As seen on TV

Coyote Blues

The hunter shot her as she fled,
drove a box nail through her head,
hung her pelt upon the wall,
where her wreckage wounds us all.

STATE OF EMERGENCY

I can feel the water pulsing through
the green rubber hose,
and all my hopes and anxieties
converge in the silvery spray—
dragging the weight from
one meager bed to the next,
day after fissured day.

I dream of oaks
and fecund roots.
I am like the choir,
praising what I cannot see
and petitioning for mercy.

Memorizing basic cloud types,
I haunt the sky for nimbostratus.

I am not a farmer or a farmer's wife.
I'm as powerless as an expectant father.

Surely though, this thirst
must count for something?

The Paved Road

The day started promising;
ended in broken glass.

III

As Close as I Can

It began in a closet. My mother made room
for her newborn in a narrow walk-in, enlivened
by a small window's glimpse of sky.

Evenings, she'd put *The Owl and the Pussycat*
and *Winken, Blinken, and Nod* on the record player,
and when the narrator purred, "Now Toni,
I'm going to tell you a story,"
I trembled with joy.

How vivid those moments
that press us into selfhood.
How golden, the sound of our name.

REALITY CHECK

You are here.

Mixed Messages

It was all a big misunderstanding. One day, over lunch and apropos of nothing, Doris said, "I've always wanted a monkey." About a month later, an opportunity arose and I bought her a capuchin. I phoned her with the news, asking if I could bring it over. "Of course," she said, "your timing's perfect." When I got there with the monkey and a year's supply of diapers, she was horrified. She'd heard *cappuccino.* "If I ever said anything about a monkey," she said, "anything at all, it was that I *never* wanted a monkey. Get that filthy thing out of here!"

The monkey lives with me now. I don't like him much, but what can you do.

Aviso

Shipwrecks of certainty
In a *wine-dark* sea—
Our advice:
Keep swimming.

Dream Job

I finally have my dream job:
Poet.
My relationship with others, however,
is at an all-time low.

A famous man I occasionally run into
reminds me he's old—that we're old.
I want to tell him it's not the being old
that's troublesome, it's the dying—but
since he doesn't mention that part,

neither do I.

Four A.M.

The hour when someone,
finding themselves awake,
wishes it wasn't so.

Weight

My ex mother-in-law gave me an anvil for
Christmas. Robert brought it over when he
dropped the kids off from their every-other-
weekend with him. "Where do you want this?"
he said. "How about the top shelf, above the stove,"
I said. "Are you kidding," he said, "this thing weighs
a ton!" "Why do you suppose your mother gave
me an anvil?" I said. "Is it some sort of metaphor?"
"How should I know," he said. The children were
jumping up and down. "Na-na, Na-na, Na-na!"
they chanted. "Just put it anywhere," I said.

Away From Here

"Bring me my horse!" I trumpet to no one in particular, knowing full well I'll have to fetch her myself. She's down at the far end of the pasture, grazing on the moist spring grass. I grab a couple of carrots, hoping to entice her to meet me halfway, but she keeps her head down, switching her tail at the occasional fly. "You love me a little bit, don't you?" I say, slipping the halter over her head. She doesn't know it, but without aficionados like me, horses would be no more than an historical footnote. "Come on, girl," I say, leading her back up the hill. "Let's go for a ride." I brush her until she shines. I sense that, even as she leans into my touch, she resents the power I have over her. She's proud and quick; a real beauty. "You love me a little bit, don't you? No? *Andale pues.*"

I Know I Know

Saying what I mean unvarnished,
on paper at least,
suits me.

When I'm with you
I go on and on.

Unreliable Witness

Now that I'm whole again,
I'm left to wonder if I wasn't better
off injured. At least I knew I existed.
While this poem's a talisman of sorts,
it betrays ignorance. I'm out of my depth.
Everything I say is suspect.

Pyrolysis

Science may explain
Why an onion
Cooks sweet—
But who can explain
Why an onion.

The Surrealist Poet

What he means to say is
He can't say what he means.
If he could, or thought he had,
He'd soon recognize his error.
But since it's his error he means to describe—
Voila!

Thing

I'm open! All I need is some _____,
some excellent _____
I can chew on/over, other than
the same old _____.

At this point (.)
I'll try any _____.

_____ is, I want to write
some _____, but it appears
I have no _____ to say.

Which came first the chicken or the egg?

Boredom, boredom came first.

Numero Uno

It was our congregation's annual Fourth of July picnic. The sun was out, the children were happy, the sky shone baby blue. We were about an hour into the festivities when Reverend Biggs approached our table. "Good day to you all," he said. "Good day to you," we said. Reverend Biggs then turned his attention to me. "Our choir would like to invite you to join its ranks," he said. "We all agree, you'd be a wonderful addition." "But I can't sing," I said. "What could I possibly contribute?" "My child," he said, "everyone can sing. My wife has a lovely voice, but to hear her tell it, she's tone deaf." "I'd rather die than perform in public," I said. "How about if you wave the baton?" he said. "Do you think you could do that?" I thought about it for a long moment. I imagined myself, my back to the audience, my hair, a bit longer than it is now, my arms outstretched, poised to release the downbeat. The anticipatory hush. "I guess we could give it a try," I said.

CAPRICE

Stop rolling, fugitive ball.
Stop immolating, tiny moth.
Stop aching, hip joint in sleeve of flesh.
Stop twitching flash point of desire—

No one can talk you out of anything.

FANCY FREE

I go into the dark,
where no one's ever been—
Everyone is there.

Year's End

When I see
how at odds
with myself I am,
I think of my fellows
and how they must
sometimes feel.
It's not that misery loves company;
our plight is our revelation.
Since god doesn't love us—
we must so do.

Ever Onward

Like the pioneers,
the dead horses,
and the smoke,

a part of us remains.

Lately, I've been outed in my dreams—
disparate masks, reparsing the past.
   The only way to tell if I'm awake or asleep
   is to walk out of the house and see if I can fly.
Yes.

Everything shines in this liminal light,
as when the eyes fill with tears.
   I don't cry as I used to. Am I more, or less, frustrated?

I attend to sleep's imaginings:
   the broken thread of self—
delinquent and disorderly,

Are we there yet?

ACKNOWLEDGMENTS

My thanks to Bill Driskill for his encouragement, Trish Reynales for her divine editing, and Jerry Rounds, as ever, for his love and support.

ABOUT THE AUTHOR

Born and raised in Los Angeles, Toni Stern enjoyed a highly productive collaboration with the singer-songwriter Carole King. Stern wrote the lyrics for several of King's songs of the late '60s and early '70s, most notably "It's Too Late" for the album *Tapestry*. The album has sold more than 25 million copies worldwide and received numerous industry awards. In 2012, *Tapestry* was honored with inclusion in the National Recording Registry to be preserved by the Library of Congress; in 2013, King played "It's Too Late" at the White House. That song and Stern's "Where You Lead" feature in the Broadway hit *Beautiful: The Carole King Musical*. "Where You Lead" is also the theme song for the acclaimed television series *Gilmore Girls*. Stern's music has been recorded by many artists, from Gloria Estefan and Barbra Streisand to Faith Hill and Drag-On. She lives in Santa Ynez, California. *As Close as I Can* is her second volume of poetry.

A Note on the Type

As Close as I Can is typeset in Spectrum, designed by Jan Van Krimpen for the Dutch printing and typefounding firm Joh. Enschedé en Zonen. Spectrum is a direct descendant of the great Aldine types of Venice, which are characterized by pen-based curves and oblique serifs.

www.ingramcontent.com/pod-product-compliance
Lightning Source LLC
Chambersburg PA
CBHW031427290426
44110CB00011B/563